Harmonica for Beg

Easy to learn and fun for travel

harmonicabreeze.com

- Basic music theory
- Learn the notes
- Songs from around the world
- Single notes and chords
- Over 90 melodies

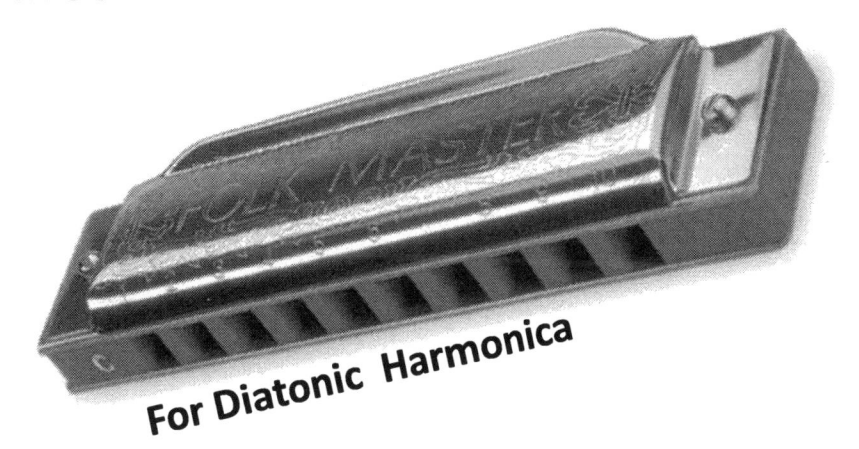

For Diatonic Harmonica

Site: www.harmonicabreeze.com

The Harmonica

Why learn harmonica

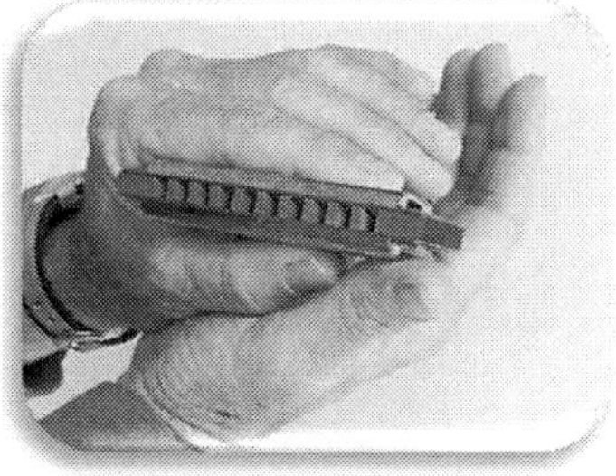

Harmonica for beginners is for any person **from 8 to 80** who likes the sound of the harmonica and wants to learn how to play.

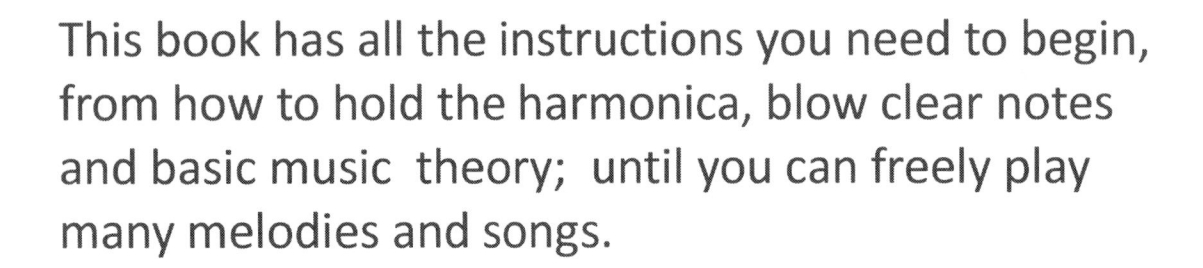

This book has all the instructions you need to begin, from how to hold the harmonica, blow clear notes and basic music theory; until you can freely play many melodies and songs.

The right way to learn and advance properly is by **practicing about 20 minutes every day** .

Do not rush! Read carefully all the instructions and advance step by step.

The best sign to move on to the next page is when you can play the songs fluently and enjoy your playing.

You've mastered a piece when you can play by ear.

Remember! It's a fun to play harmonica but you have to practice to make it happen.

Good luck!

HarmonicaBreeze - Learn To Play Harmonica 1

Get free Music tracks For the book at www.harmonicabreeze.com

Why I play the harmonica

When I was 10-year-old my mother gave me a gift - two small harmonicas, one major and one minor scale.
I started playing music and gradually I found songs that matched my harmonicas.
These harmonicas went with me everywhere, every trip and I would go and play and enjoy along the way .

When I grew up and studied music at the College of Teachers and finish my Master of Education (B.Ed. And M.Ed in Music), I realized that Each song is built off a carton scale appropriate to carton harmonica scale.
For many years I taught music and guitar lessons. I was a musician who wrote composed and arranged music for different events and my harmonica kept in a drawer.

One day a good friend turned to me and asked for help finding a harmonica teacher for her young children. Her request made me longing for the sweet sounds of the harmonica.
I told her to give me a week to think about the matter.
Within that week I found out more and more that I want to teach harmonica so my answer was positive.

I happily bought books and started teaching and learning harmonica .
To this day, many years I enjoy teaching harmonica . I play in different events and combines playing harmonica with the guitar or ukulele.
 Harmonica goes with me everywhere and I am playing in many trips for my pleasure and all the people around me.

Contents

About the Book	2
Get free music tracks	3
Introduction	5
Types of Harmonicas	6
The Harmonica to learn	7
The Diatonic Harmonica - c scale	8
Holding and Sound Producing	9
Basic care and first notes	10
Writing Notes – the Pitch	11
Writing Notes – the Duration	12
First notes C E	13
the note G	14
Practice notes C E G	15
First Songs	16
The note F	17
Eighth notes	18
Legato and Syncope	19
The note A	20
Dotted quarter note	21
The note B	22
Third interval playing	23
C - Scale (do major)	25
Dance	26
Sixteenth notes	27
The note B1	28
The note G1	29
Songs around the world	30
Songs around the world	31
Songs around the world	32
Songs around the world	33
Songs around the world	34
Songs around the world	35
Songs around the world	36
Free stave	37
Free stave	38
Musical Basic Vocabulary	39
Harmonica Breeze Site	40

HarmonicaBreeze - Learn To Play Harmonica 1

Introduction

Is this Book for you?

Harmonica Breeze is a book written for harmonica lovers from around the world.

Beginning students may find many songs and melodies from around the globe.

The lessons include music for harmonica and chords for guitar accompaniment. Some songs have tabs for the harmonica. Over 90 harmonica songs and exercises to play for diatonic harmonica.

Learn the easy way step by step with all the instructions you need. Do not rush, Take your time and enjoy your learning.

Ami Luz

Music teacher and musician. Over 30 years of teaching experience.

Completed M.Ed. for music education at Lewinsky college in Israel. Guitar teacher for more than 30 years and Harmonica teacher for the past 12 years.

Ami has written six instructional books for learning various musical instruments, including the ukulele, guitar and harmonica.

There is a new harmonica site that follows the book where you can see and hear Ami playing, play along to a video accompaniment online as well get a support and help thru the site using **contact us** and **Facebook**.

HarmonicaBreeze - Learn To Play Harmonica 1

Types of Harmonicas

Diatonic Harmonica (10 hole Blues Harmonica)
A small harmonica, comfortable for learning, built on one scale. Allows sound bending and playing basic chords. Suitable for playing blues, country, folk, and rock.

Chromatic Harmonica 12 holes
A three-octave harmonica. The chromatic button lets you play halftones so you can play all the accidentals and all of the scales. Particularly suitable for playing folk and classical music.

Chromatic Harmonica 16 holes
Professional harmonica with 4 octaves. Chromatic side button lets you play all scales. Suitable mainly for playing folk and classical music.

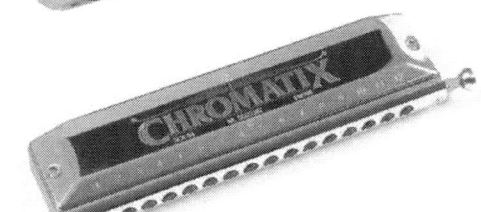

Tremolo Harmonica
Harmonica with two lines of holes, plays double tones giving music a quaking effect. This harmonica is difficult to learn to play but has a special sound.

Bass Harmonica
Accompanying Harmonica playing low tones. Suitable for harmonica ensembles. Two rows of holes allow you to play two octaves.

Chord Harmonica
Accompaniment Harmonica that plays up to 48 chords. Each chord built from 8 notes. The Most expensive and the longest Harmonica.

Mini Harmonica
The smallest harmonica. It has 4 holes and plays one octave. Suitable for hanging on the neck or keychain.

Harmonica Case
Case that contains a set of different scales diatonic harmonicas. You can purchase a set of several harmonicas in different keys for example a set of 12 or 24 harmonicas.

HarmonicaBreeze - Learn To Play Harmonica 1

The Harmonica to learn

About the harmonica

The harmonica is one of the easiest and most convenient instruments to learn. It's a small instrument so you can take it with you anywhere you go and play it anywhere and anytime.

The harmonica is the only wind instrument that can play two and more notes at the same time. That means that it is a harmonic instrument that can play both melodies and chords.

Studying at **C scale harmonica**

Diatonic Harmonica (Blues Harmonica)

We learn on the **diatonic harmonica**.
This small harmonica is comfortable to hold and easy to blow and produce the sound. It is about 7 cm in length, has 10 holes and plays three octaves. It is amazing how much sound such small and low cost Instrument can produce.

The word **diatonic** means that all the notes this harmonica can play belong to one particular scale. The type of scale is written on the side. This book is for studying
at **C scale** (written on the harmonica).

The diatonic harmonica can also **bend sounds** utilizing a special technique.
Special effects like sound bending is used for playing blues and country style.
The diatonic harmonica is comfortable to hold in a neck-holder to play with a guitar.

HarmonicaBreeze - Learn To Play Harmonica 1

Diatonic Harmonica – C scale

◱ BLOW (Exhale)

∨ DRAW (Inhale)

The notes for the harmonica are written one octave below their true pitch for ease of reading on the staff

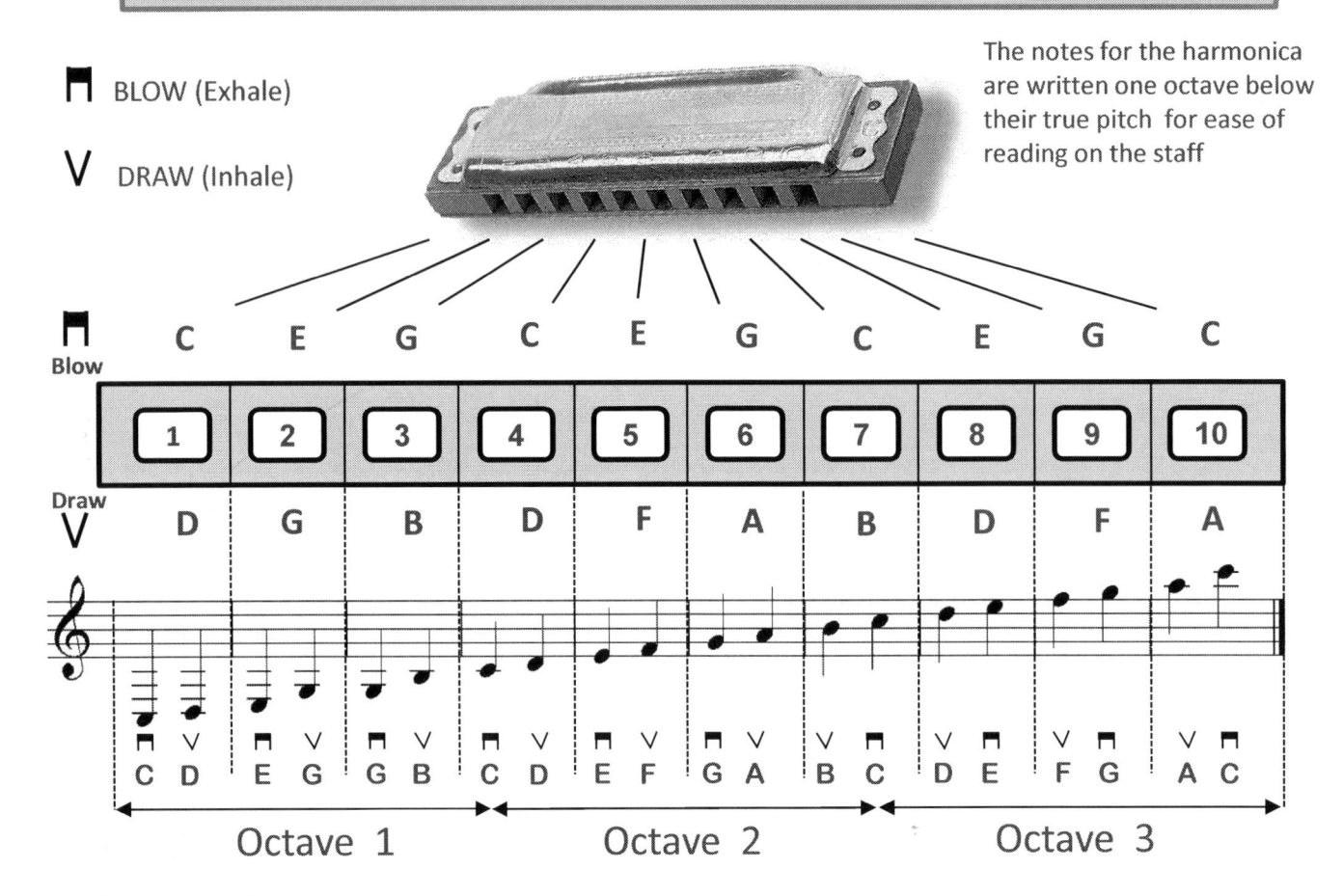

Hole	1	2	3	4	5	6	7	8	9	10
Blow	C	E	G	C	E	G	C	E	G	C
Draw	D	G	B	D	F	A	B	D	F	A

Octave 1: C D / E G / G B / C D
Octave 2: E F / G A / B C / D E
Octave 3: F G / A C

Please note !
There is no F (**fa**) and A (**la**) tones/notes on the first octave, and B (**ti**) note at the third octave. You can reach these note by note bending technique.

Some Diatonic Harmonica Scales

Key of G

Key of A

HarmonicaBreeze - Learn To Play Harmonica 1

Holding The Harmonica

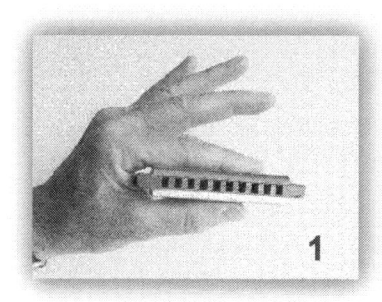

1

Diatonic Harmonica is hold at the left hand between the thumb and index finger. The numbers of the holes are on the upper side. The left will played low tones.

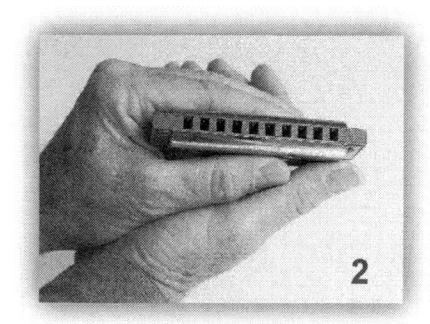

2

Close the left hand fingers as an arch, bring right hand behind the harmonica, closed fingers and create a sort of small sound box at the back, thumbs up front next to each other.

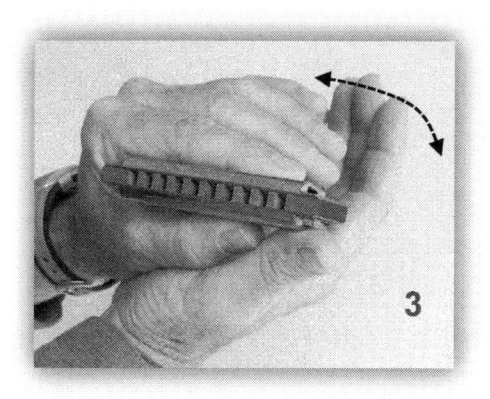

3

Create a Tremble (**Vibrato**) sound effect playing - open and close right hand fingers several times. Thumb stick together during this action.

Blowing and Sound Producing

Try these two forms of blowing and select the one convenient for you - Each method has advantages and disadvantages and the main thing is that you feel comfortable with it.

Tongue Block

Open lips, the tongue little ahead. Put your harmonica between your lips, the tip of the tongue under hole 4 and blow air pass through the center of the tongue straight. Sides of the Tongue closes the side holes softly and lips close around effortlessly.

Try to produce just one sound, don't let the air escape from the sides of your lips.

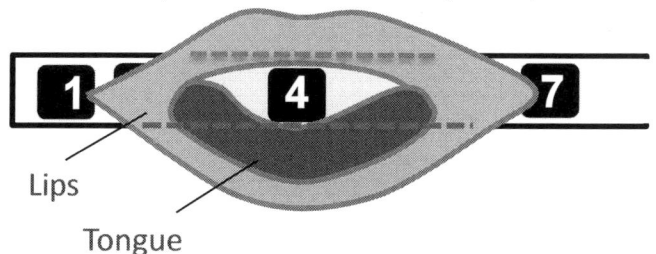

Lips
Tongue

Lips Block - pucker

Close lips gently without pressure but leave a small pinhole at center.
Easily klatch lip to the harmonica will facing hole 4 for example, and blow air.
Try to be accurate and produce just one sound. Don't let the air escape from the sides of your lips.

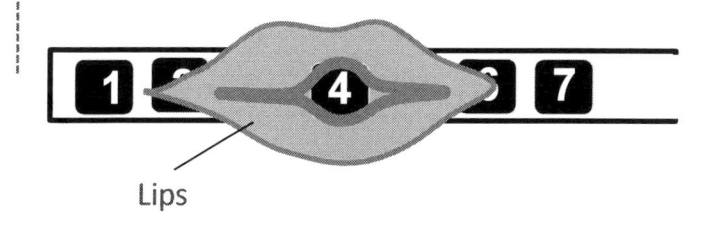

Lips

HarmonicaBreeze - Learn To Play Harmonica 1

Basic care and first notes

- ❏ Be sure to clean your mouth before playing. We recommend to rinse before playing.
- ❏ Before playing the harmonica warm it between your hands so it will play better - especially in the winter.
- ❏ At the end of playing tap harmonica holes down on the wrist or leg to remove the accumulated saliva.
- ❏ Do not touch inside the holes. The mechanism inside the harmonica that produces the sound is gentle and sensitive.
- ❏ If the harmonica sounds fake or bad try to remove the barrier by puffing a little and if that doesn't help – sent it for repair.
- ❏ After finishing playing leave the harmonica outside the case for 5 minutes to let the saliva dry out - then store it in it's case.

The First Exercises

- ❏ In the following exercises, try to get a single tone and focus. It does not come immediately. You must practice 20 minutes every day and be patient.
- ❏ In the following exercises there are hole numbers of the diatonic.
- ❏ A sign ⊓ indicates blowing air into the hole.
- ❏ Always try to keep a steady beat throughout the exercise .
- ❏ When you run out of air, lift the upper lip and take in some fresh air - continue playing without removing the harmonica from your lips
- ❏ To move from one hole to the next, move your harmonica and not your head.

Exercise A

Diatonic holes	4	4	5	5	4	4	5	5	4
	⊓	⊓	⊓	⊓	⊓	⊓	⊓	⊓	⊓

Exercise B

Diatonic holes	4	4	5	5	6	6	5	5	4
	⊓	⊓	⊓	⊓	⊓	⊓	⊓	⊓	⊓

HarmonicaBreeze - Learn To Play Harmonica 1

Writing Notes

The Pitch

- Sound can be high or low in **pitch**. Low pitched notes are played on the left side of the harmonica and high pitched notes are played on the right side.
- The **pitch** is written by drawing circles on five parallel lines. These five lines are called a staff.
- The **notes** are written as circles **on** the lines or **between** the lines of the staff.

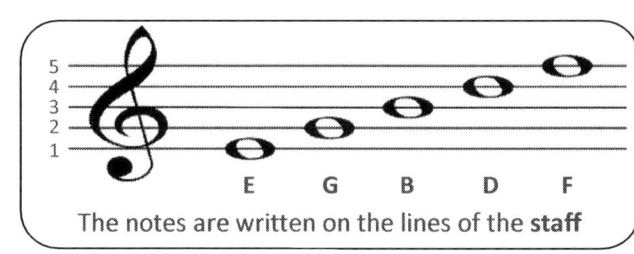

E G B D F
The notes are written on the lines of the staff

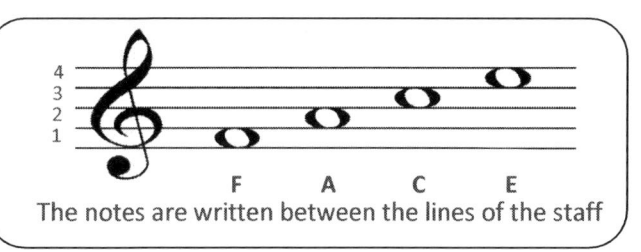

F A C E
The notes are written between the lines of the staff

G Clef

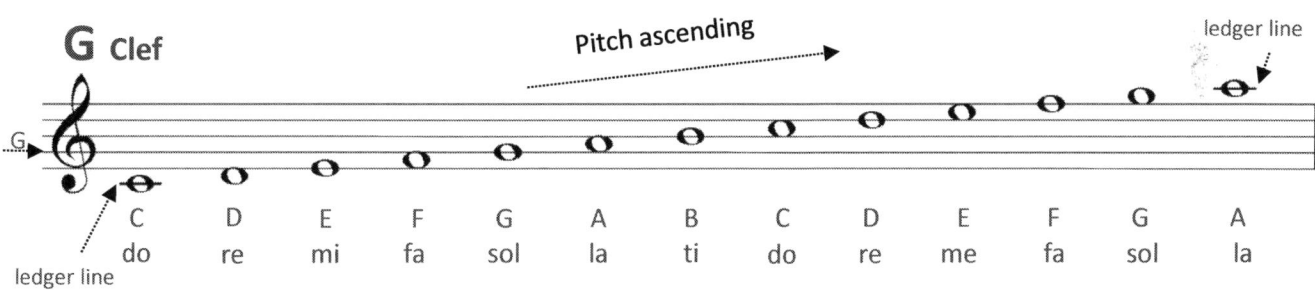

Pitch ascending →

ledger line

C D E F G A B C D E F G A
do re mi fa sol la ti do re me fa sol la

ledger line

- The Higher the **pitch** the higher the note will appear on the staff.
- Notes that are higher or lower than those that are written on the five lines of the staff will be written on **ledger lines.**

The G Clef or Treble Clef is curved around the second line of the stave indicating the location of G note. It is used for high pitched instruments like the harmonica, flute, guitar, trumpet, etc.

G Clef

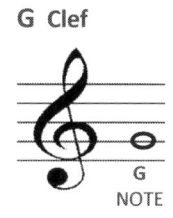

G NOTE

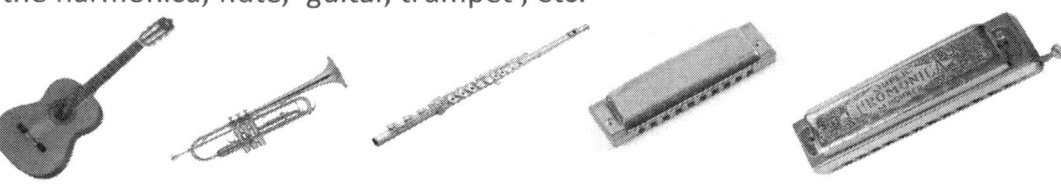

The F Clef or Bass Clef is curved around the fourth line of the staff and indicates the location of **low F**. It used for low sounding instruments such as: bass harmonica, tube, double bass, bass guitar etc.

F Clef

F NOTE

HarmonicaBreeze - Learn To Play Harmonica

Writing Notes

sound duration

Notes can be short or long in duration. The way to indicate this is by modifying the shape of the note.

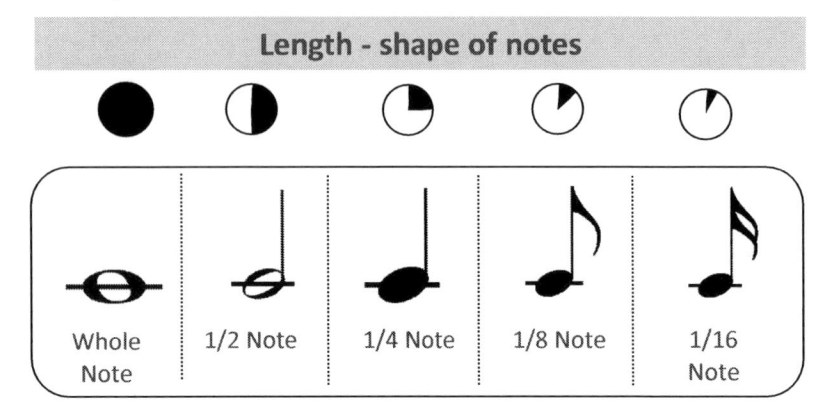

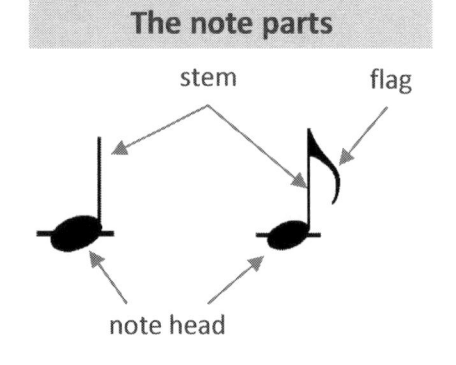

Length - shape of notes

| Whole Note | 1/2 Note | 1/4 Note | 1/8 Note | 1/16 Note |

The note parts

stem, flag, note head

We determine the duration of sounds by the beat.
In music we count beats. Every song or musical style has its own beat

BEATS are repetitive pulses at a constant rate (such as a clock ticking) and they help us to count the length of the notes. We play music according to a beat.
The speed of the beat or pulse varies from one song to another depending on the song.

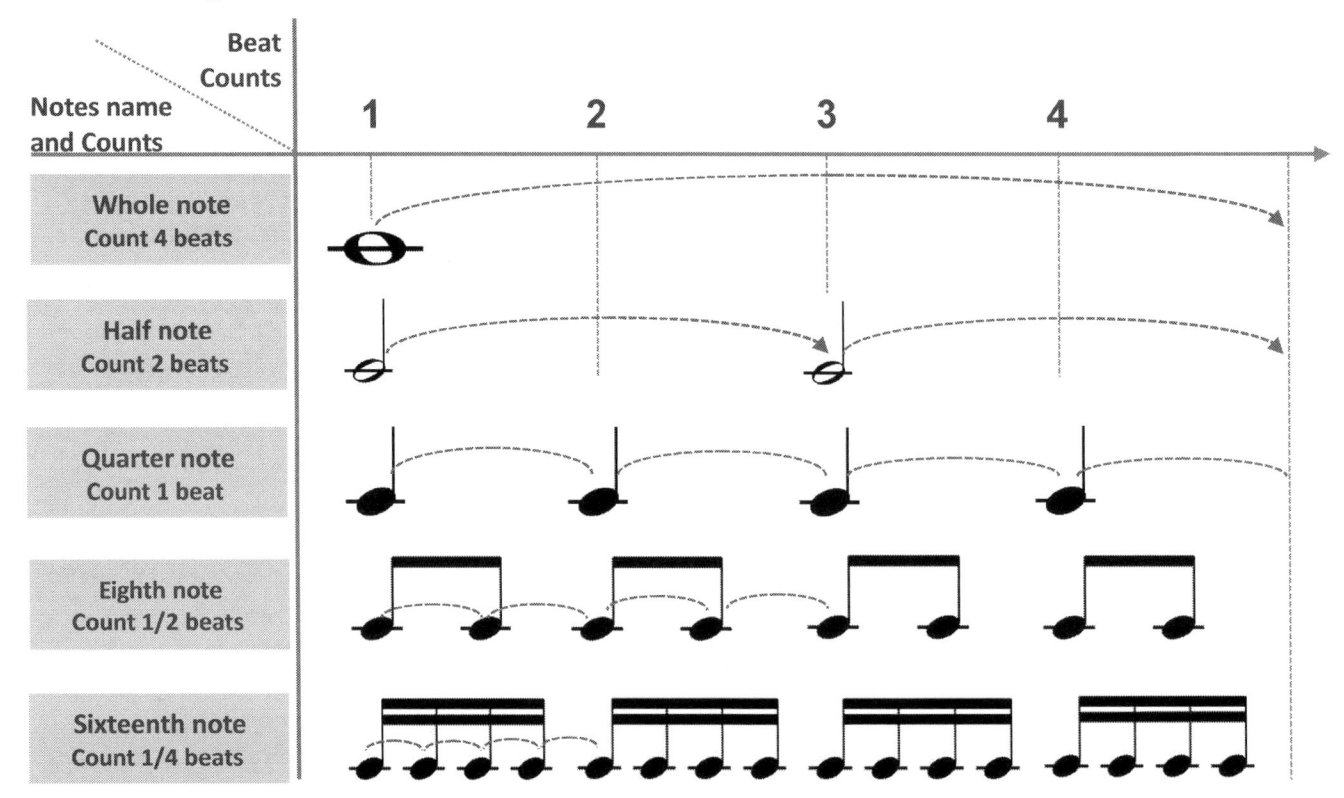

Beat Counts

Notes name and Counts: 1 2 3 4

- **Whole note** - Count 4 beats
- **Half note** - Count 2 beats
- **Quarter note** - Count 1 beat
- **Eighth note** - Count 1/2 beats
- **Sixteenth note** - Count 1/4 beats

HarmonicaBreeze - Learn To Play Harmonica

First notes

Note ! This book is made for diatonic in the Key of C

Instructions: Always try to produce one clean note, if you play a few notes together Narrow slightly the space between the lips, continue to play and in time it will work out .

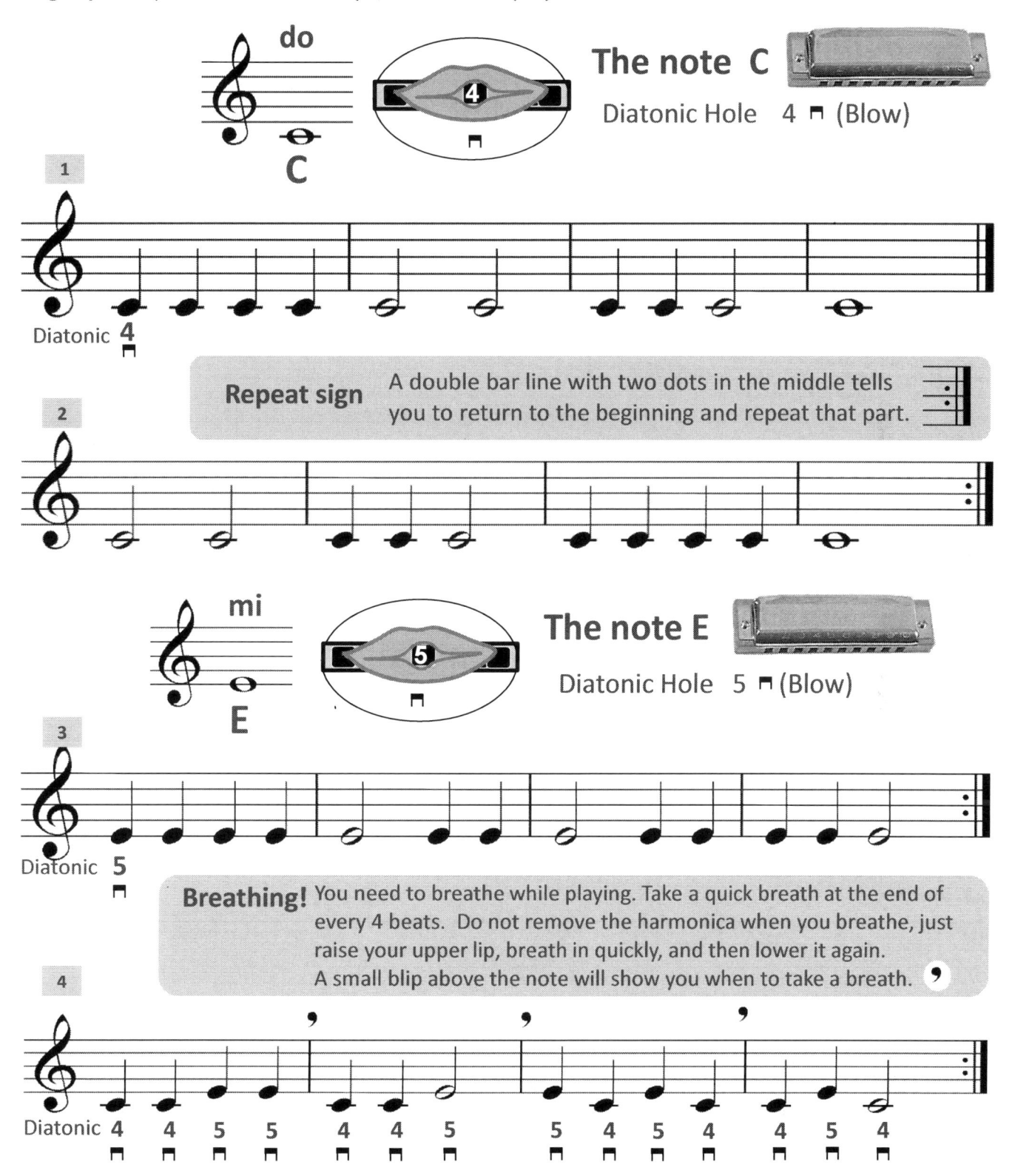

do
C

The note C
Diatonic Hole 4 ⊓ (Blow)

1
Diatonic 4 ⊓

Repeat sign — A double bar line with two dots in the middle tells you to return to the beginning and repeat that part.

2

mi
E

The note E
Diatonic Hole 5 ⊓ (Blow)

3
Diatonic 5 ⊓

Breathing! You need to breathe while playing. Take a quick breath at the end of every 4 beats. Do not remove the harmonica when you breathe, just raise your upper lip, breath in quickly, and then lower it again.
A small blip above the note will show you when to take a breath. ,

4
Diatonic 4 4 5 5 4 4 5 5 4 5 4 4 5 4

HarmonicaBreeze - Learn To Play Harmonica 1

The note G

sol
G

Diatonic Hole 6 ⊓ (Blow)

5

C C E E G G E E
Diatonic 4 4 5 5 6 6 5 5

6 **Three beats to a bar**

Measures also called "**bars**" divide the beats, or pulse of the music into groups of accented and unaccented beats. Vertical lines on the staff tell us where the measure or bar ends.

7 Bar 1   Bar line   Bar 2   Bar 3   Bar 4

Beats 1 2 3 4   1 2 3 4   1 2 3 4   1 2 3 4

Time Signature

Four **4** - Four beats in bar
quarters **4** - The quarter note gets one beat

The cycle of beats to each bar is called a **Time Signature** and is shown at the beginning of the song. The **Time Signature** has two numbers. The upper indicates number of beats count in each measure/bar, and the lower one tells us which note gets one beat.

8

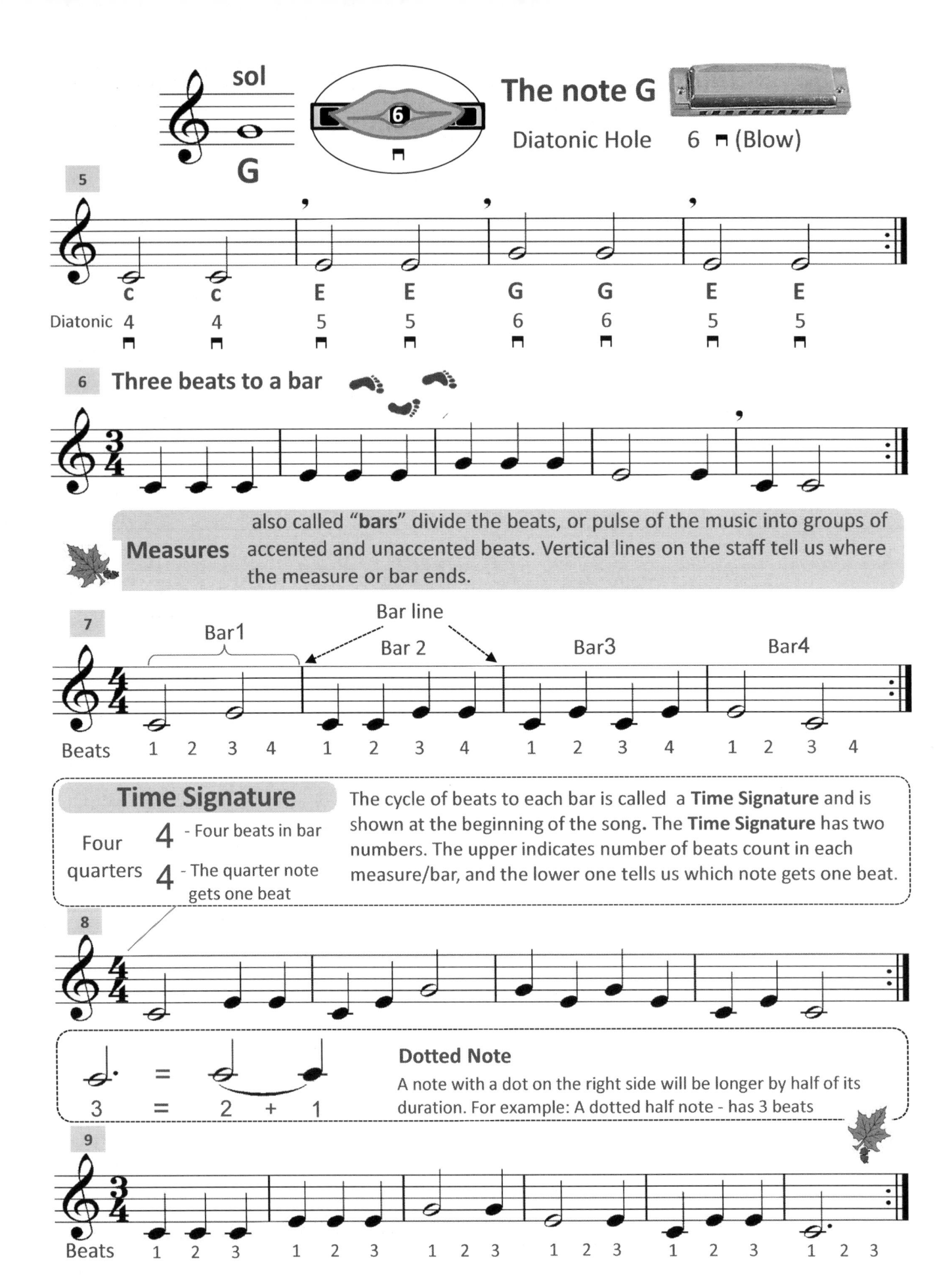

Dotted Note

𝅗𝅥. = 𝅗𝅥 + 𝅘𝅥
3 = 2 + 1

A note with a dot on the right side will be longer by half of its duration. For example: A dotted half note - has 3 beats

9

Beats 1 2 3 1 2 3 1 2 3 1 2 3 1 2 3 1 2 3

HarmonicaBreeze - Learn To Play Harmonica 1

Practice Notes   C   E   G

Play C,E,G, - blowing only. Practice each exercise until you have a clean sound and steady rhythm.
Keep in mind! Playing the harmonica requires effort but - **the more you play the less you sweat.**

10

Diatonic 4 4 5 5 6 6 6 5 4 5 6 5 4

11

12

Volta
(ending) When **the 1st ending** appears above the bar - play to the two dotted lines (the repeat sign), return to the beginning and play again but the 2nd time skip first and play the 2nd ending.

Prima Volta (play first time) Secondi Volta (play second time)

13

14

The letter **C** at the beginning of a Song indicates a four-four time, with four beats to a measure.

Vibrato - Sign to shake the sound   (See p. 9)

15

16

HarmonicaBreeze - Learn To Play Harmonica 1

First Songs

The note D

Diatonic Hole 4 ∨ (Draw)

17

Diatonic: 4⊓ 4∨ 4⊓ 4∨ 5⊓ 4∨ 4⊓ 4∨ 5⊓ 4∨ 5⊓ 4∨ 4⊓

Diatonic Harmonica Cords Accompaniment

You can accompany melodies with chords of multiple notes together. Use **C** and **G** chords on the diatonic harmonica.

C - The first four holes **Blow**
G - The first four holes **Draw**

18 Au clair de lune (In the Moonlight) *French children's song*

C   C G   C G   C

In 1876 – The inventor **T. A. Edison** recorded himself singing this song, the first recording in history.

19 Mary had a little lamb

C   C   G   C   C   C   G   C

20 Good morning

C   C   C G   1. C   2. C

21 At the dance

C   C   G   C   C   C   G   C

Staccato ♩. a point above or below the note head must played **short** and **choppy**

22 Raindrops

HarmonicaBreeze - Learn To Play Harmonica 1

The note F

fa / F

Diatonic Hole 5 ∨ (Draw)

23 A Small Scale

Diatonic: 4⊓ 4∨ 5⊓ 5∨ 6⊓ 5∨ 5⊓ 4∨ 4⊓ 4∨ 4⊓

24 A Little Etude

25 Skipping

ROUND (canon) — When two players playing the same melody but gap of beats (or time). When First player reaches **2.** the second player starts playing from the beginning **(1.)**

26 Bell Canon
French song

27 The Cuckoo
German children's song

Alegro

28 Little John (Lightly Row)
German children's song

HarmonicaBreeze - Learn To Play Harmonica 1

Eighth notes

1/4 = 1/8 + 1/8 = 1/8 + 1/8
Beats: 1 = 1 and = 1 and

One quarter is divided in to two eighths

29 Play twice. Play twice.

Duet - A musical piece for two players in 2 separate stave

30 The Eighth Duet

Player 1

Player 2

31 Walk and Run

32 Jingle Bells *Christmas holiday song*

Fast &Cheerful

C   C   F   C   1. Dm G   2. G   C

Rests

Silence, do not play but count the beats as if you are still playing

Notes Duration

Rest duration

33 When the Saints go Marching in *American Song*

Fast &Cheerful

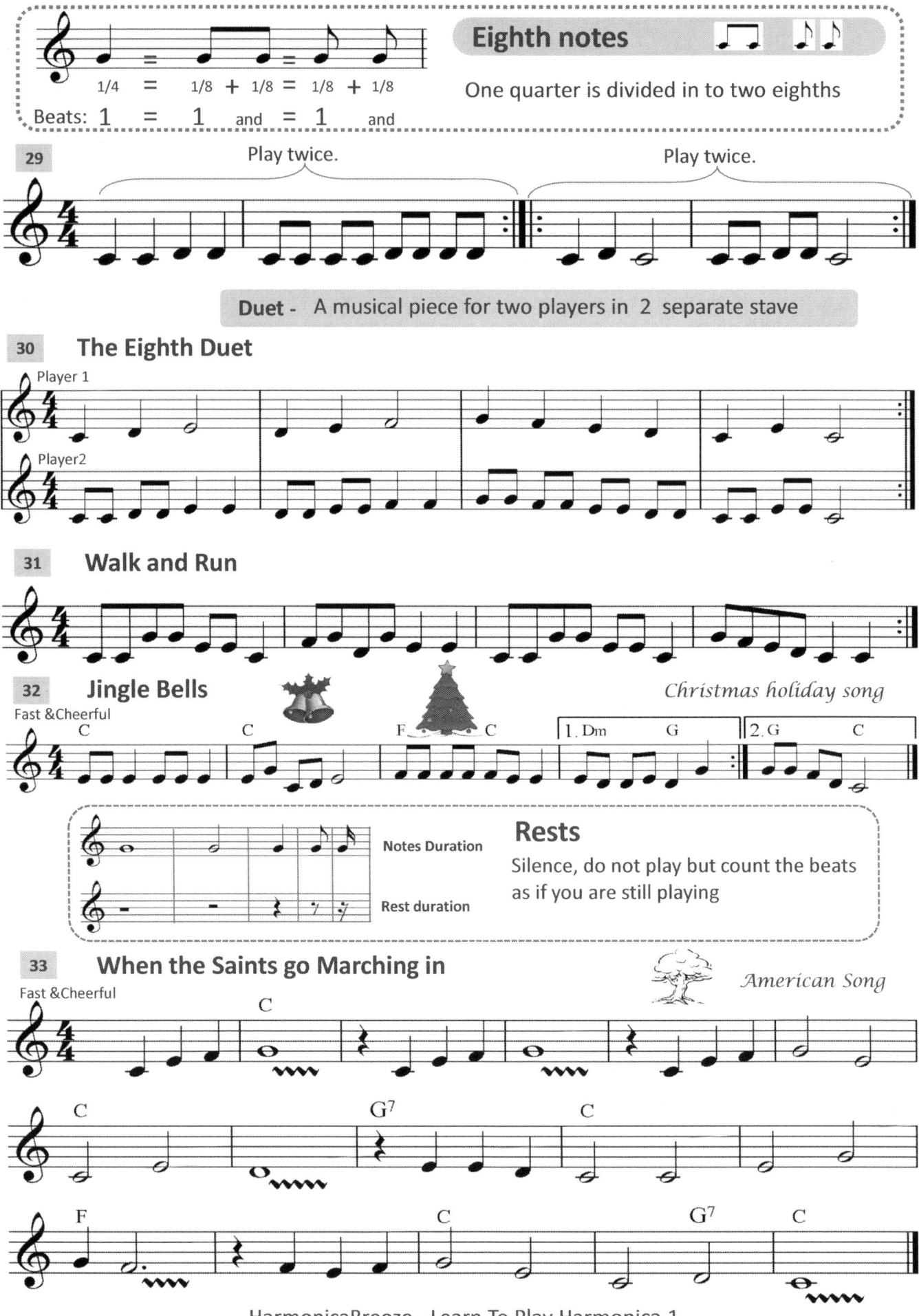

C

C   G⁷   C

F   C   G⁷   C

HarmonicaBreeze - Learn To Play Harmonica 1

34. Ode to Joy
(From the 9th Symphony) (To play quarter dotted with Eights of see p. 21) *L. V. Beethoven*

Slowly and with dignity

35. Debka
Druze dance

Fast

LEGATO — Sounds linked together, written as an arc connecting two different notes which tells you to play them as a continuous sound as smoothly as possible. Legato can only be played on neighboring holes, exhaled or inhaled. (See the example)

36. A Song in Legato
Andante

Syncopated rhythm — Rhythm pattern of: eighth, quarter, eighth notes. should play fast and easy. Found in many East European folk songs

37. Dobell Cherkasy
Cherkassian Dance

fast

HarmonicaBreeze - Learn To Play Harmonica 1

The note A

la — A

Diatonic Hole   6   V (Draw)
Chromatic Hole   7   V (Draw)

38. A.B.C.

Diatonic: 4 4 6 6   6 6 6   5 5 5 5   4 4 4   **Fine**   6 6 5 5   5 5 4   **D.C. al Fine**
□ □ □ □   V V □   V V □ □   V □ V   □ □ V V   □ □ V

D.C. al Fine (Da Capo al Fine)   Go back to the beginning and play again to **Fine**

39. David King of Israel
Easy & Cheerful   *Israeli song*

Chords: C | C F G | C | F C C | C | F G⁷ C

Fermata
Stop/Station - Appears above head of the note, allowing you to hold the note as long as you feel.

40. Au clair de la Laune (In the Moonlight)
Andante   *French children's song*

Chords: F C F C F | F | C F C F | Gm | C⁷ F | C F C F

41. Oh Susanna
Fast & cheerful   *American Song*

Chords: C | | G C | G⁷ C | F C | G C | G⁷ C C

HarmonicaBreeze - Learn To Play Harmonica 1

Dotted quarter note

1 And 2 and

A Dotted quarter lasts one and a half beats. A dotted quarter usually appears With an eighth followed and count together two beats.

42 Little Etude
Andante

43 London Bridge
Andante
English children's song

44 Air
Moderato
Mozart

45 This Old Man
Allegretto
American children's song

HarmonicaBreeze - Learn To Play Harmonica 1

The note B

Diatonic Hole   7   V (Draw)

46 Dance

Diatonic: 6 6 7   7 6 6   7 6 6   6   6 6 7   7 6 6   6 7 6   6

47 Walk in the Woods

Slow

G   Em   D   G   D   G   Em   Am   G

48 Old Macdonald

fast   *American Song*

G   C   G   D⁷   G   C   G   D⁷   G

G   C   G   D   G

Tie

A tie links between two notes at the same pitch telling you to play them as one long lasting sound.

49 Michael Row the Boat Ashore

Fast & cheerfully   *American Song*

C   F   C

C   F   G   C   G   C

Third interval playing

Third - two notes interval
playing two sounds together in the space of three steps.
A nice sound (consonant).

50 Diatonic ⊓5/4 V5/4 ⊓6/5 V6/5 ⊓7/6 V6/5 ⊓6/5 V5/4

51 Diatonic
5 5 6 6 | 5 5 6 6 | 5 5 6 6 | 5 5 6 6 | 6 6 6 | 6 6 6
⊓ ⊓ ⊓ ⊓ | ⊓ ⊓ ⊓ ⊓ | V V V V | V V V V | ⊓ V ⊓ | ⊓ V ⊓
4 4 5 5 | | | 4 4 5 5 | 7 7 7 | 7 7 7

52 Dance in pairs
moderato

53 Salterelle — Tielman Susato
Moderato
C — Dm — G — G⁷ — C
C — Dm — G⁷ — C — G⁷ — C
C — F — C — G⁷ — C

54 Salterelle (Play thirds) — Tielman Susato
Moderato

55. Drunk dancing
(Pay attention to the time signature changes) — *French song*

Allegro

56. Kol Dodi (The voice of my beloved)
Israeli song

Allegretto

57. On Top of Old Smoky
American Song

Allegretto

58. Long Long Ago
American Song

Moderato

HarmonicaBreeze - Learn To Play Harmonica 1

C Scale - do major

Now you can play all the notes in the **C major scale**, therefore many songs in one octave.

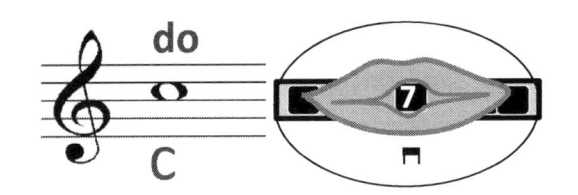

The note C

Diatonic Hole   7 ⊓ (Blow)

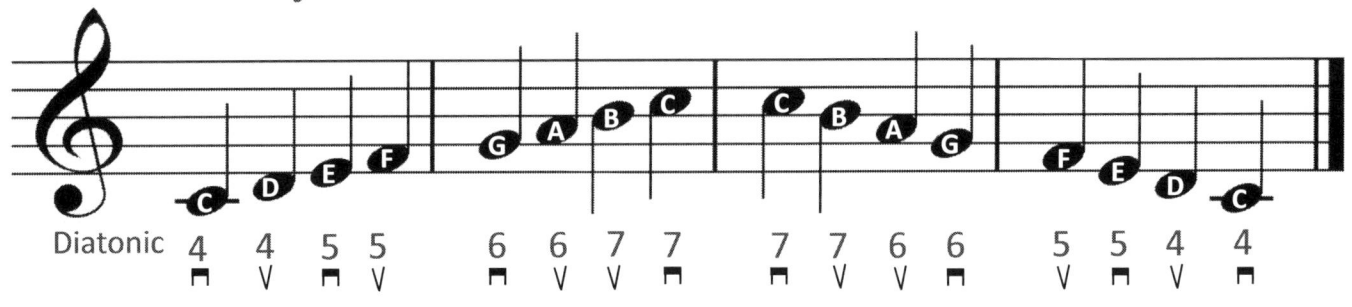

59 C Major Scale

Diatonic 4 ⊓ 4 ∨ 5 ⊓ 5 ∨ 6 ⊓ 6 ∨ 7 ⊓ 7 ∨ 7 ⊓ 7 ∨ 6 ⊓ 6 ∨ 5 ⊓ 5 ∨ 4 ⊓ 4 ∨

Music Scale
Ascending or descending sequence of tones that are used as building blocks to create melodies and musical compositions.

C Major Scale
Scale which starts with sound c (do) climb up 8 notes To high c . on piano keyboard playing on the white keys only.

One Octave
The interval between two notes that has the same name but difference of eight steps. For example C1 to C2

C Scale on the Keyboard

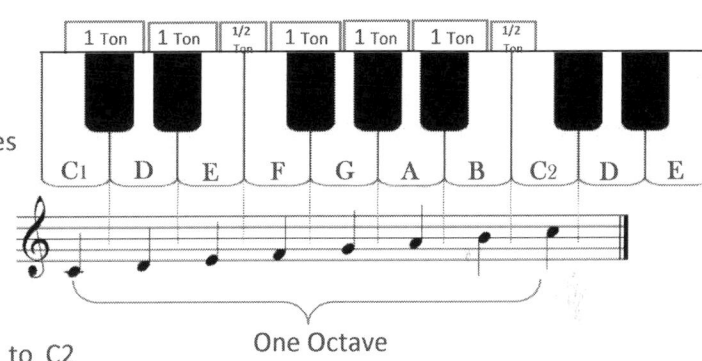

| 1 Ton | 1 Ton | 1/2 Ton | 1 Ton | 1 Ton | 1 Ton | 1/2 Ton |

C1 D E F G A B C2 D E

One Octave

60 Skipping Up   First play it without Legato.

61 Skipping Down

62 The Scale in Threes

HarmonicaBreeze - Learn To Play Harmonica 1

Dance

63 Allegro **Polka** — *Czech dance*

64 Allegro **Spring Dance** — *(Round for 2 voices)*

65 Allegro **Simi Yadech** (Give me Your Hand) — *Israeli Dance*

66 Allegro **Yesh Lanu Taish** (We have Goat) — *Israeli Dance*

Sixteenth

Rhythmically - one quarter is divided into two-eighths and four sixteenths
I.e. playing 4 notes on one beat
Play slowly at first until you get used to the rhythm of the music.

67 A Game of Rhythm

68 Debke dance
Allegro
Druze folk dance
Fine
D. C. al Fine

69 Hanukah Hanukah
Allegro
Jewish holiday song

HarmonicaBreeze - Learn To Play Harmonica 1

27

The note B

B Low
ti

Diatonic Hole 3 V (Draw)

---

70 Allegretto **Minuet** *J. S. Bach*

71 Andante **Polly Wolly Doodly** *American Song*

72 Allegro **Krkovyak** *Polish dance from Krakov*

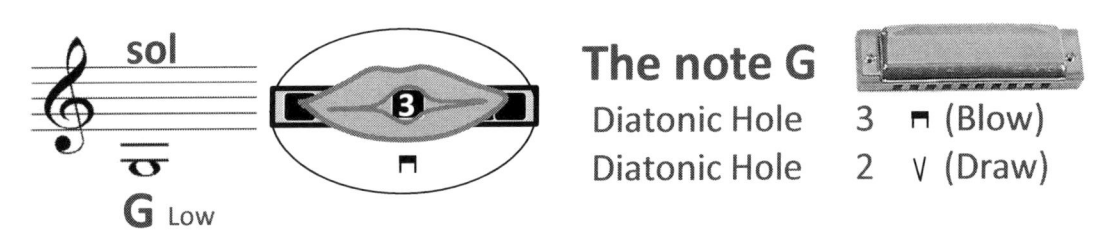

The note G

sol — G Low

Diatonic Hole 3 ⊓ (Blow)
Diatonic Hole 2 ∨ (Draw)

For **Diatonic harmonica** we prefer playing the note G hole 3 blow rather than note G hole 2 draw.

73. First Sol

Diatonic: 4 3 3 3 | 4 3 4 5 | 4 3 3 4 | 4 3 4
         ⊓ ∨ ⊓ ∨ | ⊓ ∨ ⊓ ⊓ | ⊓ ∨ ⊓ ∨ | ⊓ ⊓ ⊓

74. Canon Cuckoo
Allegro — Holland Song (Round for 2 voices)

75. The Happy Farmer
Allegretto — Schumann

HarmonicaBreeze - Learn To Play Harmonica 1

76. Down in the Valley
Moderato — American Song

77. Inky Dinky Parlez - Vous
Allegretto — French and American song

78. Boi da cara-preta
Adagio — Brazilian Lullaby

79. The Spring
Moderato — Mozart (Round for 3 voices)

D.C.

80. She'll be Coming Round the Mountain
Allegro — American Song

HarmonicaBreeze - Learn To Play Harmonica 1

81 **La Cucaracha** Mexican Song

Moderato

The note in the Brackets is for Diatonic Harmonica

82 **The Spring** W. A. Mozart (Round for 3 voices)

Moderato

83 **Minuet** J. S. Bach

moderato

HarmonicaBreeze - Learn To Play Harmonica 1

84 Oh My Darling Clementine　　　　　　　　　　　　　　　　　　　　*English song*
Moderato

85 Jug of Punch　　　　　　　　　　　　　　　　　　　　　　　　　　*Irish song*
Moderato

86 Boogie-Woogie　　　　　　　　　　　　　　　　　　　　　　　*American dance*
Moderato

HarmonicaBreeze - Learn To Play Harmonica 1

87 Little Maiden

Allegretto

Brazilian song

88 God Save the Queen (British Anthem)

Moderato

English song

89 Um die Muhle

Moderato

Slovak song

D.C.

90 Aleuette
Allegretto

French children's song

Fine

D.C. al Fine

91 The Marines' Hymn
Allegro

American March

Fine

D.C. al Fine

92 Come to the Sea
Allegro

Italian song

HarmonicaBreeze - Learn To Play Harmonica 1

93 Carnival in Venezia

Italian song

Moderato

94 **Believe Me If All Those Endearing Young Charms**

Irish song

Free stave for you

Glossary of musical terminology

Dynamics - relative volume level in music

PP - pianissimo - very soft/quiet

P - piano - soft / quiet

mp - mezzo piano - somewhat soft

mf - mezzo forte - somewhat loud

f - forte - loud / strong

ff - fortissimo - very loud

Cres. Crescendo
getting louder

dim. Diminuendo
getting softer

Tempo - the speed of the music (BPM- beat per minute)

adagio - slow - 66 – 76 (BPM)

andante - walking speed - 76 – 108 (BPM)

moderato - medium speed - 108 – 120 (BPM)

allegro - fast - 120 – 168 (BPM)

presto - very fast - 168 – 200 (BPM)

acc. accelerando
growing faster

rit. ritardando
getting slower

○ One ton bending

C major scale two octaves

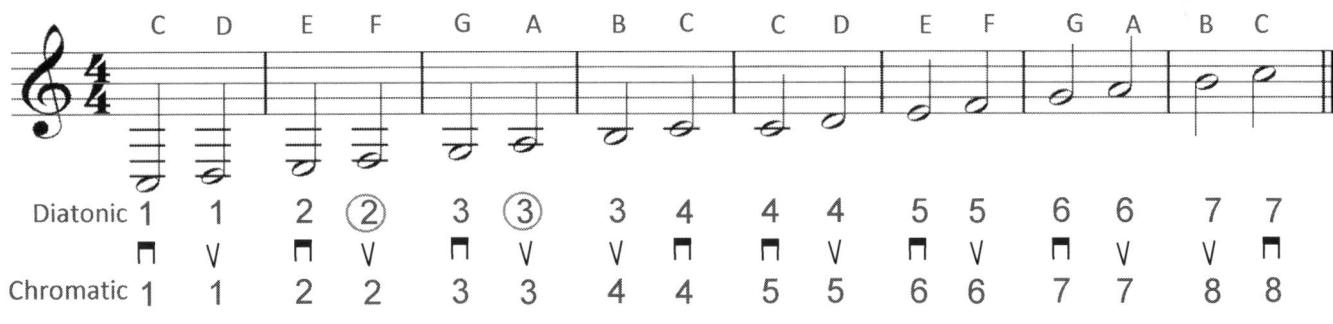

	C	D	E	F	G	A	B	C	C	D	E	F	G	A	B	C
Diatonic	1	1	2	②	3	③	3	4	4	4	5	5	6	6	7	7
	⊓	V	⊓	V	⊓	V	⊓	⊓	V	⊓	V	⊓	V	V	⊓
Chromatic	1	1	2	2	3	3	4	4	5	5	6	6	7	7	8	8

A minor scale two octaves

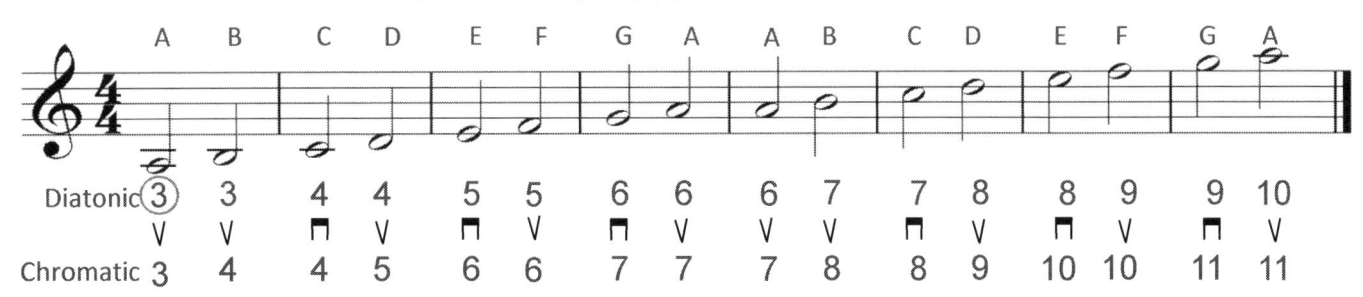

	A	B	C	D	E	F	G	A	A	B	C	D	E	F	G	A
Diatonic	③	3	4	4	5	5	6	6	6	7	7	8	8	9	9	10
	V		⊓	V	⊓	V	⊓	V	V		⊓	V	⊓	V	⊓	V
Chromatic	3	4	4	5	6	6	7	7	7	8	8	9	10	10	11	11

HarmonicaBreeze - Learn To Play Harmonica 1

Harmonicabreeze.com
Site accompanies this book

Each lesson contains video clips

Get teacher help thru mail or face book

Free lessons to try

The next Book - **Harmonica for Advanced**

When you hold a Harmonica,
a whole world of music is in your hands
Use it anywhere you wish

Ami Luz

Good luck

Printed in Poland
by Amazon Fulfillment
Poland Sp. z o.o., Wrocław